First World War
and Army of Occupation
War Diary
France, Belgium and Germany

63 (ROYAL NAVAL) DIVISION
Royal Marine Brigade
9 Chatham Royal Marine Battalion
26 August 1914 - 12 October 1914

WO95/3108/2

The Naval & Military Press Ltd
www.nmarchive.com
Published in association with The National Archives

Published by

The Naval & Military Press Ltd

Unit 10 Ridgewood Industrial Park,

Uckfield, East Sussex,

TN22 5QE England

Tel: +44 (0) 1825 749494

www.naval-military-press.com

www.nmarchive.com

This diary has been reprinted in facsimile from the original. Any imperfections are inevitably reproduced and the quality may fall short of modern type and cartographic standards.

© Crown Copyright
Images reproduced by permission of The National Archives, London, England, 2015.

Contents

Document type	Place/Title	Date From	Date To
Heading	WO95/3108-2		
Heading	BEF France 63 (Naval) Division R Marine Bde 9 Chatham Bn 1914 Aug-1914 Oct		
War Diary	Chatham	26/08/1914	26/08/1914
War Diary	Ostende	27/08/1914	30/08/1914
War Diary	Sheerness	31/08/1914	01/09/1914
War Diary	Freedown (St. Margarets Bay)	18/09/1914	18/09/1914
War Diary	Dunkerque	19/09/1914	30/09/1914
War Diary	Cassel	03/10/1914	03/10/1914
War Diary	Antwerp	04/10/1914	04/10/1914
War Diary	Lierre	04/10/1914	06/10/1914
War Diary	Antwerp	07/10/1914	08/10/1914
War Diary	Redoubt Line Antwerp	08/10/1914	08/10/1914
War Diary	Antwerp	08/10/1914	09/10/1914
War Diary	St Giles Waes	09/10/1914	09/10/1914
War Diary	Blankenburg	09/10/1914	10/10/1914
War Diary	Ostende	11/10/1914	11/10/1914
War Diary	Dover	12/10/1914	12/10/1914
Operation(al) Order(s)	Operation Order No 1 by Brig Gen A Paris Commanding Royal Marine Brigade	04/10/1914	04/10/1914
Miscellaneous	To O.C. No. 1 & 3 Coys		
Miscellaneous	From Brigade Commander. To O.C. No. 1 & (CH) Battalion.		
Miscellaneous	Operation Order No. 1 by Lieut. Col. C. Mc N. Parsons, O.C. 9th Bn. R.M. Brigade.		
Map			

WO 95/31018 (2)

WO 95/31018 (2)

BEF FRANCE

63 (NAVAL) DIVISION

R. MARINE BDE

9 CHATHAM BN

1914 AUG — 1914 OCT

Copy of

Copy of the Diary

WAR DIARY.

DARDANELLES

9th Battn. R.M.L.I. (later Chatham Battn. R.M.L.I.)

August 1914 - July 1915.

	1914. Aug.	
CHATHAM.	26th a.m.	Battalion embarked at SHEERNESS in H.M.S. "Euryalus" having left Chatham Dockyard in Tug. Brig. Genl. Aston came on board and assumed command of R.M. Bde.
OSTENDE.	27th a.m.	Landed at OSTENDE. An outpost line was taken up round OSTENDE 9th(Ch) Bn. on N.E. of the town extending from the coast on left to BASSIN de CHASSE (?) on the right. Bn. H.Q. at Training Stables.
	30th	Belgian troops arrived from England by transports. 4000 and 16000 (approx.) 31 Oct. & 1 Sept.
SHEERNESS.	31/1 Sept.	Embarked in H.M.S. "Prince George" and proceeded to England. Transferred to Tug in Sheerness and disembarked at Chatham Dockyard.
FREEDOWN (St. Margarets Bay)	18th noon	Marched from Freedown (St. Margarets Bay) to DOVER and embarked in "City of Liverpool"
DUNKERQUE.	19th	Disembarked at DUNKERQUE went into billets. Bn.H.Q. Hotel St. Jean. Encamped on CHAMP de MANOEUVRE. Gen. A. Paris assumes command vice Aston (sick)
	30th	Entrained at 11 a.m. for CASSEL, arriving there 1 p.m. Marched to Casino and billetted there.
CASSEL.	3rd Oct.	Entrained for unknown destination. At DUNKERQUE sidings 80 men of St. John's were waiting and entrained, being attached to 9th Bn. R.M.L.I.
ANTWERP.	4th 1 a.m.	Arrived at Station (? VIEUX DIEU) a suburb of ANTWERP and detrained. Met by Lt.Col. H.D. Farquharson, R.M.L.I. who instructed battaion to march to EDYGHEM to billets. Arrived there about 2.30 a.m. and went into billets.
LIERRE.	4th 9 a.m.	Marched out of billets and moved on LIERRE. En route were inspected by the Rt. Hon. Winston Churchill. On arrival at LIERRE took up a position in accordance with Operation Order No.1. by Brig.Gen. A. Paris, Commanding R.M.Bde. Copy attached. This line was being shelled by hostile 5.9" and Shrapnel "universal". Major Shubrick's Co. (A) and Capt. Welch's (C) were posted in advance on the river NETHE opposite LIERRE and entrenched. The remainder of the battalion were in the main defence line some 300x in rear in the Belgian trenches which were some 6' broad and 3' deep. There were no "dug-outs". The hostile fire was directed by 'Sausage" balloons which were up all the time. The Shrapnel searched for the Belgian field artillery which was very efficiently screened about 300x? to rear of the defence line while the Howitzer searched the trenches and possible Head Qrs. in woods, farms and groups of houses. Such trenches as lay through small gardens and orchards where the parapets were screened by branches and debris escaped attention, while the obvious portions were heavily bombarded. About this time a Section or so of R.E. under Capt. Rooke, R?E.

LIERRE.	4th 9 a.m.	and Lieut. is attached to the Bn. The R?E. carry out some demolition of houses in LIERRE which afford cover to the enemy to fire on our advanced positions at point blank range across the canal, or canalized river surrounding LIERRE on the North.
LIERRE.	5th	During the night 4/5 Oct. enemy brought field guns into LIERRE opposite A & C Cos. to about 400x range. In accordance with orders from Bde: O.C. Bn. ordered retirement of these Cos. to main defensive line. A Co. casualties 1 Officer (2nd Lt. A.R.Chater) and 37 other ranks. A Co. posted in support in ditch west of ROUTE D'ANVERS adjoining Bn. H.Q. This H.Q. was in the trench line at junction of 9th and 11th Bns. on ROUTE D'ANVERS. Some hostile scouts crossed NETHE and kept up rifle fire down the street on our barricade.
	6th	Hostile shelling increased in intensity. Casualties included Lt. & Qmr. J. Hammond and Colr.Sgt. Marshall (wounded). (During this (?) day Col. Marchant assumed command of R.M.Bde. and Brig.Gen. Paris command of R.N.D., the Naval Bdes. having arrived at ANTWERP) Confidential orders preliminary to retirement received about noon. Later p.m. verbal orders received that the Bn. is to retire to an intermediate line about BOSCHHOEK - EGGERSEEL - VREMDE, where Belgian Engineers are digging a defensive line. The retirement is conducted in good order. Lieut. Rutherford's Co. "D" Co. forming a Rear Guard. The troops were heavily shelled during the retirement, but there was no apparent infantry pursuit. A line was taken up by the R.M.Bde. under orders of O.C.9th Bn. on general line above mentioned. Bns. in order from the right from ROUTE D'ANVERS: 9th, 11th, 10th & 12th Bns. There was no hostile action during this time. A Naval Bde. was on the right of the 9th Bn.
ANTWERP.	7th 3 a.m.	According to orders received the R.M.Bde. retired into billets at Cinema Film Factory, CHATEAU ROUGE, WAESDONK, inside the fortified line of ANTWERP and rested there. As the factory was considered dangerous if bombarded, the men were bivouacked in the fields adjoining for the night 7/8th.
	8th 2 a.m.	Lieut. Cuttin and platoon despatched to take charge of Bridge of boats across the SCHELDT in the event of retirement through ANTWERP.
	7 a.m.	9th Bn. ordered to relieve Belgian troops on Redoubt line from SCHELDT to Redoubt No.16 inclusive. Copy of orders attached.
REDOUBT LINE ANTWERP.	8th 9.30 a.m.	Bn. arrived in position about 9.30 a.m. The Blegian Bn. 5th, declined to be relieved as they had no orders to that effect. The 9th Bn. therefore reinforced them where they were weak and took position according to orders attached. During the day huge columns of smoke rose all round ANTWERP said to be caused by burning petrol and oil stores ignited by orders of the Belgian authorities.

	p.m.	
	7.30	Major Sketchley, G.S.O.3. R.N.D. brought verbal orders that the Bn. was to retire through ANTWERP and cross the SCHELDT by the Bridge of Boats and march by ZWYNDRECHT to entrain at BEVERENWAES. About 8 p.m. the Belgian infantry retired.
ANTWERP.	8.30	The Bn. moved as ordered. Little military formation could be maintained on account of the darkness and throngs of refugees carts and transport of all kinds. The Bn. transport, 3 motor lorries were obliged to drop their ammunition into the river before crossing the bridge. Petrol was flaring round the bridge on both banks of the river and the bridge was becoming charred.
	9th.	On reaching BEVEREN WAES the Bn. was met by Gen. Paris who ordered a further march to ST.GILES WAES, as the enemy had either cut the line, or captured the trains at the former place.
ST.GILES WAES.	a.m. 4.0	From 4.8 a.m. the Bn. entrained as trains became available and proceeded to (a) BLANKENBURG (b) OSTEND.
BLANKENBURG.	p.m. 6.0	Details of 9th Bn. R.M.L.I. and 2nd R.N.Bde. detrained and requsitioned food and billets. 790 Officers and men. Lt.Col. Parsons in command.
	10th 1 p.m.	The troops proceeded by light railway to OSTEND where the various commands were re-organized. Lt.Col. Parsons assumed command of R.M.Bde. Troops billetted in OSTEND Railway Station.
OSTENDE.	11th	Among those found to be missing at OSTENDE were Lt. & Qmr. J. Hammond 9th Bn. R.M.L.I. He had been taken wounded into ANTWERP to some Hospital unknown, and was later taken prisoner by the Germans. Capt. E.J.H.Morres, 9th Bn. R.M.L.I. attached to R.M.Bde. Staff. He was interned in Holland. Capt. Rooke, R.E. Interned in Holland. Subsequently escaped to England. Lieut. R.E. Interned in Holland. Subsequently escaped to England.
		Bde. Staff R.M.Bde. & 9th Bn. R.M.L.I. embarked in S.S."Honorious" for ENGLAND, arriving DOVER about 5 p.m. 12th Oct.
DOVER.	12th	S.S."Honorious" left DUNKERQUE ROADS at 10.45 a.m. having been held up by fog during night 11/12th Oct. Arrived DOVER p.m.

Approximate State 9th Bn. to 10th Oct.

Present	554.
Missing	29.
Killed and wounded	50.
Total	633.

Copy No. 3.   Operation Order No. 1.
                              by
                     Brig. Gen. A. Paris
                  Commanding Royal Marine Brigade.

Reference Map Scale $\frac{1}{40000}$ Near R of ROUTE D'ANVERS
                                                      ANTWERP.
                                                    4 Oct. 14.

1. Information.
   (a) Belgian Advanced posts along River NETHE were engaged with German patrols last night.
   (b) Belgian artillery near LINTHE is engaged with enemy on the south side of the NETHE today.

2. Intention.
   The Royal Marine Brigade and 7th Regt. Belgian Infantry will hold the line of defence from LISP to the road junction just north of HOF VAN LACHENEN.

3. The Royal Marine Brigade and 7th Regt. Belgian Infantry will relieve the 27th Regiment now holding the above line at 11 a.m.

4. Sections:- The line to be held will be divided into sections as under
   No.1 Section (Lt.Col.DELORBE, 7th Infantry Regt)
       From road junction near L just north of HOF VAN LACHENEN to the DE of CHEMIN DE FER railway line, inclusive. E. of TURNHOUT.
   No.2 Section (Col.Parsons, 9th Bn. R.M.L.I.)
       From DE of CHEMIN DE FER railway line East of TURNHOUT exclusive to the bend of the road 400 yards S.E. of K of KLAPLAAR exclusive.
   No.3 Section (Col.Matthews No.11 Bn. R.M.L.I.)
       From the road running S.E. of KLAPLAAR inclusive to the road near DE of DE PLAS FME. exclusive.
   No.4 Section (Col.Beith No.12 Bn. R.M.L.I.)
       From the road just south of D in DE PLASFME inclusive to the river at LISP.
   Each Section Commander will form his own local reserve.

5. ADVANCE POSTS. Each Section Commander will push out advanced posts to the river and arrange to resist any movement of the enemy across the river. These advanced posts will be strongly entrenched and communication established between them and the main line.

6. RESERVES The Reserve will consist of:-
   (a) The 1st Carabiniers, who will remain on the left of the outpost line.
   (b) The 10th Battalion, R.M.L.I. at the R of ROUTE D'ANVERS
   (c) Machine Guns of Royal Navy Air Dept. at the R of ROUTE D'ANVERS.

7. ARTILLERY. The artillery groups will remain in their present positions. These positions will be communicated confidentially to Section Commanders who will take steps to get into touch with artillery commanders in thier Sections of Defence.

8. ROYAL ENGINEERS. The Royal Engineers Detachment will place the advanced posts in a state of defence.

9. In case of an attack in strength, the position of the main line will be held at all cost.

10. No smoking, lighting fires or cooking will be allowed in the advanced posts.

11. The countersign is ARLON.

12. Section Commanders will submit rough sketches of their dispositions to the G.O.C. by 4 p.m.

13. REPORTS. Reports to the House NORTH of the road near R in ROUTE D'ANVERS.

(Signed) Geo. S. Richardson,
Major,
Staff Officer.

Copy No. 2. to O.C. 7th Belgian Regt. for G.O.C.
3   O.C. 9th Bn. R.M.L.I.
4   O.C. 10th Bn. R.M.L.I.
5   O.C. 11th Bn. R.M.L.I.
6   O.C. 12th Bn. R.M.L.I.
7   O.C. Artillery.
8   O.C. 1st Carabiniers.
9   G.O.C. in C. 5th Division.

To O.C. No.1 & 3 Coys.

Be prepared for heavy bombardment, it will do little harm if you are well dug in.

G.O.C. attaches great importance to clearing field of fire. Standing crops should be cut down before dawn and all preparation made to withstand infantry attacks.

All troops should stand to arms at 5 a.m.

Two brigades of the Naval Division are expected to join us tonight. Brigadier General Paris will command the Division, and Col. Marchant, C.B., A.D.C. the R.M. Brigade.

H.Q., R.N.D. Field Force
   Route d'Anvers.   (Signed) W.H.P. Richards.
                                                   Adjt.
                                           2.10 a.m. 5.10.14.

From Brigade Commander.
To O.C. No. 1 (CH) Battalion.

      The enemy are threatening our right flank. You are to proceed with your battalion and occupy the line of trenches from REDOUBT to RIVER inclusive.

      The Belgian troops now in that position will form a reserve behind you.

                   B/O

              (Signed) M.C.Festing.
                        Capt.B.M.

5.35 a.m.
8.9.14

Operation Order No.1 by
Lieut. Col. C. Mc N. Parsons,
O.C. 9th Bn. R.M.Brigade.

Ref. Sheet 3.   REDOUBT 18.

Thursday 8.10.14.

1. A few Uhlan patrols have been reported during the morning in the direction of PUERS.

2. The 9th Bn. will reinforce the Belgian troops (5th Bn.) between Rte. du SUD and Rte. 18 and Rte 17 and Rte 16.

3. At 10.35 a.m. Companies will move as follows:-
   No.1 Co. to trench immediately E. of Rte. du SUD.

   No.2 Co. to trench immediately W. of Rte 18.

   No.3 Co. (less 2 platoons) to trench immediately East of Rte. 17.

   Two Platoons of No. 3 to trench immediately West of Rte. 16.

   No.4 Co. as local reserve at Fort No.8.

   Bn. H.Q. at small redoubt about B.5.

4. Dressing Station about Farm Buildings about B.5.

5. Position of M.G. will be detailed later.

6. A line of electric live wire running south of the first lot of barbed wire must be avoided. Care must be taken that no one is electrocuted.

7. Stores will be sent to CROSS ROADS B.4.

8. Every effort is to be made to improve the trenches to provide cover from artillery bombardment and to provide overhead cover. Communication must be kept up and all should know the position of Units and the way to reach them.

                                    (Signed) W.H.P.Richards.
                                         Capt. & Adjt. 9th Bn.
                                         10.15 a.m.
Issued verbally to O.C. Companies.

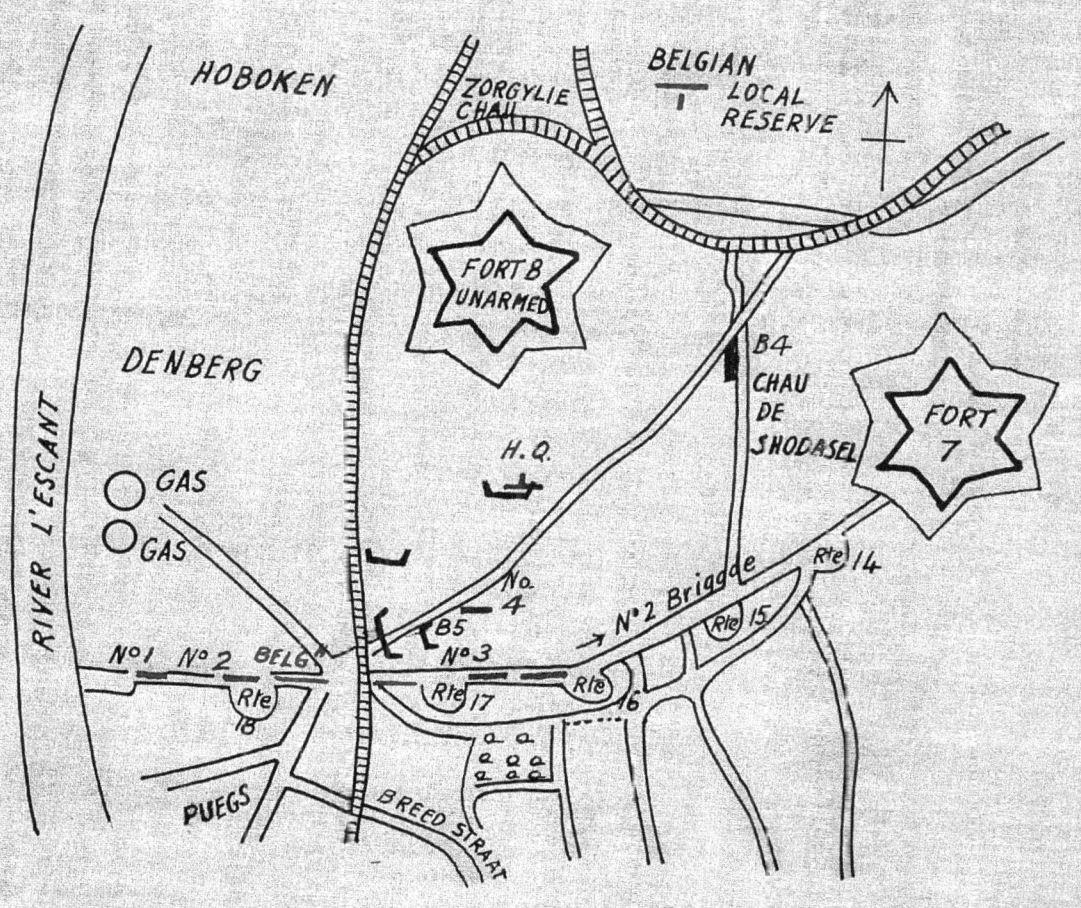

www.ingramcontent.com/pod-product-compliance
Lightning Source LLC
Chambersburg PA
CBHW081517160426
43193CB00014B/2718